KEN GRIFFEY JR.

The Boy Who Became
A Baseball Legend

In the quiet town of Donora, Pennsylvania, a young boy named George Kenneth Griffey Jr. was born on November 21, 1969, into a family that lived and breathed baseball. His father, Ken Griffey Sr., was a talented outfielder who played for the Cincinnati Reds and was part of their legendary Big Red Machine in the 1970s.

From the moment he could hold a bat, Ken Griffey Jr. was swinging for the fences. His backyard was his own personal ballpark, where he would spend countless hours practicing his swing.

As Griffey grew, so did his love for the game. He went to Archbishop Moeller High School in Cincinnati, Ohio. While there, he showed everyone what an amazing baseball player he was. He had a batting average of .478 and hit 17 home runs in two seasons of high school baseball.

Griffey was named the best high school baseball player of the year in 1987. His combination of speed, power, and defensive prowess quickly caught the attention of scouts and coaches.

On June 2, 1987, the Seattle Mariners selected Griffey with the first overall pick in the Major League Baseball draft. It was a momentous occasion, not just for Griffey but for his family and supporters who had been with him every step of the way.

Soon after, on June 11th, he joined the Bellingham Mariners, a team in the Northwest League. On June 16th, he stepped onto the field for his very first game.

In his debut season, which lasted 54 games, Ken hit .313, smacked 14 home runs, drove in 40 runs, and even stole 13 bases! His skills caught the eye of many, including Baseball America magazine, which named him the top prospect in the league.

The following year, in 1988, Ken moved up to the San Bernardino Spirit in the California League, where he played 58 games. Later in the season, he earned a promotion to the Vermont Mariners in the Eastern League. Though he only played 17 games, Ken hit.279 with two home runs and drove in 10 runs.

On April 3, 1989, Griffey's hard work and perseverance paid off as he made his long-awaited Major League debut with the Seattle Mariners. As he stepped onto the field, Griffey felt a surge of excitement and anticipation wash over him. He was determined to make the most of every opportunity that came his way.

For 11 amazing seasons with the Seattle Mariners, from 1989 to 1999, Ken was one of the most exciting players of his time! During that time, he amassed an incredible 1,752 hits, smashed 398 home runs, drove in 1,152 runs, and stole 167 bases.

Ken's talent shone brightly as he led the American League in home runs four times! And in 1997, he won a special award called the A.L. MVP, which means Most Valuable Player. Additionally, he had a super high batting average of .297 throughout his whole career.

But it wasn't just his hitting that made Ken famous. He was also an amazing defender in center field! He won 10 Gold Glove awards in a row from 1990 to 1999 for his awesome fielding skills. Ken could make the most incredible catches, diving all over the field to stop baseballs.

One of the coolest things about Ken's time with the Mariners was when he played with his dad, Ken Griffey Sr., in 1990 and 1991. They were the first father-son duo to play on the same team at the same time! They even hit back-to-back singles and home runs together.

On February 10, 2000, something big happened. Ken was traded to the Cincinnati Reds! After the trade, Ken signed a super big contract with the Reds. It was worth $112.5 million and lasted for nine years, with an option for a 10th year. Ken Griffey Jr. was ready for a new adventure in Cincinnati.

But as Ken started playing with the Reds, something changed. People noticed that he wasn't playing as amazingly as he used to. Injuries started bothering him, and he had to miss a lot of games.

In 2005, something special happened. Starting on May 1st, Ken was back in action and feeling healthy! He hit an amazing 35 home runs that season, his highest since he first joined the Reds.

Ken's hard work paid off, and he moved up the career home run list. He passed famous players like Mickey Mantle, Jimmie Foxx, and Ted Williams. It was like climbing a ladder of baseball greatness!

But even superheroes like Ken can get hurt sometimes. In September, he strained a tendon in his left foot. So, he decided to take a break from playing to have surgery on his knee and to fix scars from an old injury.

Even though he had to sit out some games, Ken still played in more games than he had in a long time. And guess what? He was named the National League Comeback Player of the Year for his amazing comeback!

In 2006, Ken continued to make history. He hit his 537th home run, passing Mickey Mantle on the all-time list. Then, after coming back from a knee injury, he hit a walk-off home run to win a game against the Washington Nationals. What a hero!

Ken didn't stop there. He kept hitting home runs left and right, tying and passing other baseball legends like Mike Schmidt and Reggie Jackson. Even when he broke his wrist on holiday, he didn't let it stop him.

In 2007, Ken hit some incredible home runs. On May 10th, he hit his 569th home run, tying Rafael Palmeiro for ninth place on the all-time home run list. Just a few days later, he passed Palmeiro and kept climbing higher and higher.

In June 2007, Ken returned to Seattle for the first time since leaving the Mariners. The fans gave him a huge welcome, and Ken was touched by their support. He even hit two more home runs during that series, adding to his impressive record.

Ken finished the 2007 season with 593 career home runs and was honored as an all-time Rawlings Gold Glove winner for his exceptional skills on the field. He showed everyone that even when things get tough, he's still one of the greatest players in baseball history!

On April 4, 2008, Ken made history by driving in his 1,702nd run, surpassing Reggie Jackson for 16th place on the all-time list. Then, on June 9, Ken smashed his 600th home run! The fans from both teams rose to their feet, cheering and applauding Ken's incredible achievement.

On July 30, 2008, in his final game for the Reds, Ken hit his 608th career home run, leaving a lasting mark on his time with the team.

On July 31, 2008, Ken Griffey Jr. began a new chapter in his baseball career as he joined the Chicago White Sox. In his very first game wearing the White Sox jersey, he showed his talent by getting 2 hits in 3 at-bats, bringing in 2 runs, and even earning a walk and scoring a run himself!

The most memorable moment was on September 30, 2008, during the last game of the season. It was a crucial match between the White Sox and the Minnesota Twins to break the tie atop the AL Central. In the fifth inning, Ken made a perfect throw, helping the White Sox win 1–0 and advance to the 2008 American League Division Series.

Despite his remarkable contributions, the White Sox decided not to keep Ken for the next season, making him a free agent for the first time in his career. On February 18, 2009, after a lot of thinking, Ken Griffey Jr. signed a contract with the Mariners, especially because the fans there always cheered for him.

Ken's return was exciting. In his first game back in April, he hit a home run against the Minnesota Twins. It was his eighth Opening Day home run! Then, on April 15, he made history by hitting his 400th home run as a Mariner and his 613th overall. Ken's leadership and fun personality helped bring the team together.

During the season, he hit more milestone home runs, like his 621st against the Yankees in July. In August, he even won a game with a run-scoring single against his former team, the White Sox.

In 2010, Ken came back for another year with the Mariners. Although he struggled at first, he still made big plays. In May, he won a game against the Blue Jays with a run-scoring single, marking the end of his amazing career in Major League Baseball.

From his humble beginnings to his legendary career filled with record-breaking moments, Ken's story teaches us about the power of perseverance, dedication, and passion for the game. As you turn the final page of this book, may the lessons from Ken Griffey Jr.'s journey inspire you to chase your own dreams with the same passion and enthusiasm.

Made in the USA
Las Vegas, NV
29 October 2024

10679281R10021